I JUST WANT TO BE *Free*

I JUST WANT TO BE *Free*

V.L.

From the 9-to-5 to the entrepreneur to the non-traditional worker, experience the joys of life through freedom in the workplace

Copyright © 2024 Victoria Jarvis
All rights reserved.
ISBN- 9798333824653

FOREWORD

Like many of you, Victoria was trapped in an endless cycle of working toxic and captivating 9 to 5 jobs. Although destined to be an entrepreneur she let the fear of failure and the unknown trap her mind and prevent her from pushing forward into her life purpose. After leaving one of the most toxic jobs she had ever had, it finally clicked that she needed to stop running from her purpose and lean heavily into her calling in life – a calling to free others from society's prisons.

As she began revisiting the various areas she could make an impact, one area stood out to her; whether it was helping women display their inner beauty on the outside through personal styling, or helping friends, family, and co-workers alike leave their toxic workplace, she quickly realized that she needed to be the voice, the whisper, that says "You're better than this, you deserve more, be free!" With those thoughts and actions in mind "I Just Want to be FREE" was born.

After years of watching friends, family, and co-workers suffer in a job that doesn't align with their personality type, their interests, or their purpose, Victoria had finally had enough and decided to write a book outlining how to get out and be free. Unlike other self-help or "leave your 9 to 5" books, "I Just Want to be FREE" is a book designed to help its readers discover what job is ideal for them, based on their personality, interests, and worker type.

Victoria believes that all worker types are valuable in society; be it the 9 to 5er, the entrepreneur, or the non-traditional worker, true freedom is found in being in your ideal worker type, utilizing your personality to excel in that role, and working in a field that brings your joy.

With this book, she hopes that you too can experience freedom in the workplace. She hopes that when you wake up in the morning you are excited and passionate about what the day will bring. And most of all, she hopes that you will have a new outlook on work-life balance and see that it is truly possible to have freedom in the workplace.

Thank you for entrusting Victoria with something so personal and important as finding freedom in working.

INTRODUCTION

Have you ever scrolled through social media, hoping to relax after a long day of work, only to be bombarded by so-called "financial gurus" screaming that you need to march into your boss' office, throw your keys on the desk, and slam the door behind you - never looking back? Do the wheels in your mind begin to turn when you see photos and videos of people taking mid-year vacations or talking about how they are free to spend time with their family and friends without worrying whether or not their job will be there when they return? Have you ever stopped to wonder; *am I being held prisoner by my place of work? Am I a slave to this toxic 9 to 5 life? Can I actually have a life where I can enjoy working?* If these thoughts have ever crossed your mind, this book is for you.

Maybe you're the 9 to 5er looking for a job that will allow you the ability to excel in your role while also giving you the necessary time off to spend with friends and family. Maybe you're the entrepreneur, tired of working for corporations that don't value your ideas or drive to make a change. Or maybe, you're a non-traditional worker, wishing you could use your skills and talents within your home to create a space that will help your family succeed in their life's purpose. Whatever category you fall into, this book is designed to help you identify if you are being held captive by your place of work, which worker type you are, and how to thrive in that area.

Gone are the days of working ridiculous hours, long drives, pointless meetings, and endless emails. You've taken the first step in experiencing workplace freedom by picking up this book and committing to change. I am so excited to go on this journey with you, and I can't wait for you to experience what true freedom in working really looks like.

TABLE OF CONTENTS

Chapter 1
The Overwhelming Desire for Freedom

-

Chapter 2
Defining Your Worker Type

-

Chapter 3
The 9 to 5er

-

Chapter 4
The Entrepreneur

-

Chapter 5
The Non-Traditional Worker

-

Chapter 6
*Setting the Foundation
(The 9 to 5er)*

-

Chapter 7
Landing the Job & Thriving

-

Chapter 8
*Setting the Foundation
(The Entrepreneur)*

-

Chapter 9
In Order to Succeed, you MUST Overcome

-

Chapter 10
*Setting the Foundation
(The Non-Traditional Worker)*

-

Chapter 11
Finally Free

CHAPTER 1
The Overwhelming Desire for Freedom

There are so many so-called "financial gurus" on the internet claiming to have the key to "financial freedom" or "quitting your 9 to 5". They promise that if you storm into your boss' office, slam your keys on the desk, and march out - never looking back - that suddenly, you'll be free from the captivities and burdens of work. It sounds exciting, thrilling, and empowering! But have you ever asked yourself, "Is this what you want? Do I want to be free from the "captivity" of working this job, or are the TikTokers and influencers I am seeing swaying me to want to leave?"

Sure, seeing so many people on the internet "up" and quitting their jobs without a care in the world is quite exciting. It's invigorating to watch young and old throw their workplace keys out of the window, never looking back at that awful 9 to 5 they have escaped from. As exciting as all of this sounds, you're hesitant. You're thinking, "Well, yeah. I'd love to be like those people. They seem to be experiencing some sort of freedom, and I'd love to get in on that, but…." Let me stop you there. Do you know if you "actually" want to be free from your job, or is the exciting world of influencers, Tiktokers, and Youtubers in fact, influencing your decisions?

Let's take a moment to delve deeper into this concept with an engaging exercise. It's time to determine whether your desire for freedom is a genuine truth or a subtle influence from the world around you. Answer the following questions:

- Am I being held captive by my current work?
- How am I being held captive?
- Do I need to be "free" or adjust?
- Do I ACTUALLY want to be free?

A person in their mid-thirties has worked for a retail company for several years. They have proven time and time again that they are fully capable of handling more responsibility. Eager to take the next step, this individual sat down with their manager and expressed a readiness to move into a leadership role. After recounting their quarterly achievements and above-average performance, the manager responded by stating that they were, in fact, not ready for the role and should continue to work towards it over the next several months. For several years, this person watched as others were promoted and outside candidates filled leadership roles. It became quite apparent that they were trapped in an endless cycle of hard work with little to no payoff.

Does this sound like you? When you wake up in the morning, are you constantly bombarded with the harsh reality that no matter what you do, no matter how hard you work, your current employer will not acknowledge your existence? Do you read work emails with frustration, knowing that if you were in charge, you could have resolved this situation already? Does coming to work bring forth a feeling of dread and despair? If you answered "yes" to any of these questions, you are currently being held captive by your place of work and in desperate need of workplace freedom. However, if you said "no" to all of these questions yet feel burdened by your employment, you may need a few career adjustments.

Certainly, being free from all types of work isn't the answer, so what exactly do you need freedom from? You need to be free from the seemingly endless cycle of overworking with little to nothing to show for it. You need to be free from continuously investing your most precious asset, time, into something that doesn't bring you joy, fulfillment, or excitement.

"Am I being held captive by my work?"

When we talk about freedom in the workplace, this does not necessarily mean freedom from working in its entirety. We are all made to contribute to society and fulfill our life's purpose through some type of work. Freedom in the workplace means being able to experience the joys of life through a fulfilling and purposeful place of work. It means utilizing your God-given skills and talents to help others and contribute positively to society. True workplace freedom is being able to enjoy working. It's working to live, not living to work.

CHAPTER 2

Defining Your Worker Type

Did you know that understanding your worker type is the key to unlocking workplace freedom? It's not just about the job you do but how you thrive in that role as well. Some find their sweet spot in a traditional 9 to 5 job, others in the freedom of entrepreneurship, and some in the unique challenges of being a stay-at-home spouse/parent. No matter your worker type, the path to self-discovery is the same.

Jeremy has been working a 9 to 5 data entry job for the past ten years. Although he does a fairly decent job, he is often unmotivated during work and depressed afterward. On his days off, Jeremy enjoys playing Madden video games, leading fantasy football leagues, and hosting flag football tournaments for his nephews. After years of monotonous and frustrating work, Jeremy decided to make a change. He took the first step in workplace freedom by discovering his personality type through a personality assessment. To his surprise, the personality assessment indicated that he has an extroverted personality with hints of type-A tendencies.

Are you like Jeremy? Do you have a job that you are good at but brings nothing but frustration and misery every time you go to work? Maybe you have a personality type and situation similar to Jeremy's; you work in a closed office where each person has a separate cubicle – a small three-wall workspace where you are alone, with no one to bounce ideas off of, no one to talk to about the weekend, and no one to share exciting life events with, and yet, you have a very extroverted personality. Although you are good at your job, your job contradicts your personality type. It's no surprise that you feel miserable and trapped…YOU ARE! It is crucial that you choose a career or industry that aligns with who you are as a person. Here are a few personality assessments that I recommend. These tests will help you understand yourself and what things/activities make you feel the most fulfilled in life.

- Myers Briggs Personality Assessment
- The Predictive Index
- Enneagram Personality Test
- Big Personality Test

Now that we know what our personality type is, we need to determine if we belong in the 9 to 5, entrepreneur, or non-traditional worker type. To do this, we must ask ourselves a series of essential questions. On the next page, you will find a little assessment to help you determine your worker type. Be as honest as you can be in this assessment. There are no wrong answers. Once you have completed the evaluation, we will begin talking about the different worker types and how the results of the personality assessments relate to them.

START

Do you like a structured environment?
- YES → Do you prefer to make ALL of the decisions?
- NO → Do you prefer to work from home?

Do you prefer to make ALL of the decisions?
- YES → Do you like to work with others?
- NO → Do you like consistency in your job?

Do you like consistency in your job?
- YES → Can you easily leave work at work?
- NO → Do you like to work with others?

Do you like to work with others?
- YES → Do you value spending time with family over getting paid?
- NO → You are an Entrepreneur

Do you value spending time with family over getting paid?
- YES → You are a Non-Traditional Worker
- NO → Do you feel that work has a deeper meaning than getting paid?

Do you prefer to work from home?
- YES → Can you easily leave work at work?
- NO → Does change bother you?

Does change bother you?
- YES → Does having a manager or overseer bother you?
- NO → You are a 9 to 5er

Can you easily leave work at work?
- YES → Do you value spending time with family over getting paid?
- NO → Do you feel that work has a deeper meaning than getting paid?

Does having a manager or overseer bother you?
- YES → Do you feel that work has a deeper meaning than getting paid?
- NO → You are a 9 to 5er

Do you feel that work has a deeper meaning than getting paid?
- YES → You are an Entrepreneur
- NO → You are a 9 to 5er

You are a 9 to 5er

You are an Entrepreneur

You are a Non-Traditional Worker

CHAPTER 3

The 9 to 5er

I once had a manager who said, "Everyone says it's better to work for yourself than for someone else, but sometimes, it might be better to be an employee rather than your own boss." Surprisingly, I agree with her! What a strange thing to read in a book all about "freedom in the workplace," right? But hear me out; for some people working for a company where they can come between 9 am and 5 pm, do their job, and go home is ideal. They like the structure of a work environment, the consistency of knowing exactly what the following workday will entail, the socialization of like-situated individuals, and the comfortability of not being the one making all of the tough decisions. For the sake of understanding, let's call these people the "9 to 5ers". If this sounds like you, then you are a 9 to 5er, and you should absolutely continue working for some organization or company. "But Victoria," I hear you saying, "I want to be free too!" Don't worry, this book is also for you!

Freedom as a 9 to 5er can vary from person to person; it all depends on your personality type, what you enjoy, the ideal work environment, and why you value working for someone over working for yourself.

What You Enjoy

At the beginning of the book, we discovered our personality type and which worker category we most identify with; let's now talk about what activities we find most enjoyable in our lives. There is an old saying that goes, "If you do something that you enjoy, you'll never work a day in your life," and that is precisely what we are going to accomplish here.

Remember our friend Jeremy? After completing the personality assessment, he discovered that he has an extroverted personality with a hint of type A. Based on his personality type, Jeremy would thrive in an environment that lets him plan, coordinate, and organize events and activities. As an extrovert, being around and working with people is something that he will find enjoyment and fulfillment in. Jeremy also loves sports, specifically football. He enjoys playing Madden video games, leading fantasy football leagues, and hosting flag football tournaments for his nephews.

Take some time to think about what you enjoy. Are you a foodie? Do you like to travel? Do you love art? Does building things sound fun to you? Whatever it might be, use the spaces on the next page to write down a few things that bring you joy in life that, if you could get paid to do, you would.

"If you do something that you enjoy, you'll never work a day in your life."

The Ideal Work Environment

When working a 9 to 5, the work environment is almost as important as the job itself. Many employees have stated that the reason they love their job rarely relates to their position but rather to the people they work with and the overall atmosphere.

Two retail clothing stores have offered you the visual manager role. Company A is a well-known department store, and Company B is a smaller, lesser-known store that is still quite profitable. Company A has offered you a $100k yearly salary, a 9 am to 5 pm M-F schedule, and a detailed training package to help you accurately execute the visuals in their store to their standards. Company B has offered you a $75K yearly salary, the flexibility to choose your schedule, so long as you meet the required 40 hours a week, and the autonomy to execute the store's visuals as you deem fit, ensuring that it aligns with the brand's aesthetic. At company A, corporate leaders are harsh and rigid. They are not open to creative feedback and often berate the visual and department managers during their visits. They are known to swear at in-store management and belittle leaders in front of their subordinates. Company B's executive team, however, often praises well-executed visual sets by sharing said photos throughout the company. Should a leader need to be corrected, upper management makes it a point to contact the individual privately and have a closed-door, yet respectful, conversation with them. The in-store team at company A is visibly miserable. They don't like their job, leaders, or customers, but when asked why they stay, they respond, "Because of how much I make here. Nowhere else is hiring at these rates. I hate it here, but I might as well stay." At Company B, the in-store team appears to be full of life and happy. They get along, and everyone seems to love what they do. When asked why they stayed, they responded, "I absolutely love working here! The executive team is kind and understanding. They set clear expectations and goals for us, and they provide us with resources to set us up for success. Although I don't have the highest salary in my field, I have the freedom to set my own schedule and my regional manager is flexible if something unexpected happens. It's a great job!"

Between the two companies, which would you work for? In our 9 to 5 search, we want to look for companies whose employees are happy. Employees who have nothing but great things to say about their leaders and the overall environment. We are looking for current employees who feel heard and respected and former employees who left on good terms with the company. If the 9 to 5 job you are looking at doesn't align with these things, consider looking elsewhere. If your current employer is anything like the toxic example above, consider this your sign to find a new place of work ASAP.

Annoyed with his current place of work, equipped with a deeper understanding of himself & his personality type, and a love of sports, Jeremy decided that enough was enough and that it was time to make a change. He knows that working in closed spaces, like a cubical, is not something he is interested in. However, the idea of an open floorplan whereby he can interact with co-workers sounds like a dream. One of the things about his data entry job that he did not like was how rude and unrealistic his supervisors were. Jeremy desires managers and executives with realistic timelines and goals in his new role.

Use resources like Glassdoor, LinkedIn, current and past employee feedback, and other online reviews to help you learn about ABC company's work environment. Let's do a little exercise: In the lines below, write down a few things you desire in your ideal work environment and some things that are immediate turn-offs.

Ideal Work Environment	Horrible Work Environment

Working for Someone vs. Being Your Own Boss

As a 9 to 5er, you have determined that you prefer to be an employee rather than your own boss, but why? Why would you rather work for someone else rather than be for yourself? "Victoria," I hear you saying, "What a silly question. Because it's easier!" But is it really "easier"? Every job has its ups and downs, difficulties and simplicities, risks and rewards; so, what is it about working for someone else that makes you say, "I'd rather be a 9 to 5er than an entrepreneur or a non-traditional worker"? While you think about your answer, let me tell you what my former co-worker said when faced with the same question.

When talking with my former co-worker about the benefits of working for someone else, she said, "I like the stability of it. Many small business owners and entrepreneurs live in a constant state of not knowing when their next paycheck is going to come. Maybe they get the bulk of their money at the beginning of every month, or maybe they are having a tough year, and sales have been lower than they could have predicted. I, personally, cannot live in such a constant state of uncertainty. Additionally, I like that I can focus on ONLY doing my job and what I enjoy. As a W2 employee, I don't have to figure out health insurance, business taxes, or employment law. I am free to come to work, do my job, and leave knowing that all those logistical things are already taken care of. For me, I can be entrepreneur-minded within my 9 to 5."

So, what about you? Why do you prefer to be a 9 to 5er rather than your own boss? Is it the company insurance? The PTO benefits? The ability to work with the same people daily? The consistent paycheck? What is it about the 9 to 5 that you find so beneficial that you want to stay in this worker type?

In Jeremy's case, he thrives in a structured environment. Coming to work, knowing precisely what is required of him, was the only saving grace for his data entry job. Yes, he is a planner, and he can host. Yes, he has a strong ability to connect with people, but

"Why would you prefer to be a 9 to 5er rather than your own boss?"

he loves doing his job ONLY. The various sub-tasks that come with being an entrepreneur seem dull to him. For Jeremy, a job within an open floor office space centered around sporting events with realistic and obtainable goals is the perfect 9 to 5 job.

In Chapter #6, we're going to combine all of the tools we have acquired in this chapter and use them to leap into workplace freedom. In the meantime, continue pondering what you have learned in this chapter, and maybe you'll pick up some helpful tips as we continue with the entrepreneur worker type.

CHAPTER 4
The Entrepreneurs

"Be your own boss" has been a phrase plastered all over social media since 2020. From small business owners to entrepreneurs to social media influencers and YouTubers alike, the concept of ditching your 9-to-5 and working for yourself has become more than just a trend; it has become a way of life.

The road to entrepreneurship varies from person to person, but like the 9 to 5ers, it all starts with a personality assessment.

Jennifer works as a pet groomer at a well-known pet store. Long ago, she took a personality assessment that indicated that her personality is introverted with elements of creativity, caregiving, and innovation. Based on the assessment results and her love of animals, Jennifer thought being a pet groomer was the best career choice for her. Getting hired at the pet store was so exciting for her. The news filled her heart with joy and excitement for the next chapter in her career. After six months of working, Jennifer started feeling frustrated and hatred for her job. "How can this be?" She thought, "The personality assessment was spot on, and I love my furry clients. How can I have so much hate towards a job that is seemingly perfect for me?"

Does this story sound familiar to you? Maybe this is you. You've taken the personality assessments, spoken to the life coaches, read the books, and taken the courses. Still, for some reason, after a short period, you become annoyed and dissatisfied with your place of work. No matter how many companies you work for or how many times you change jobs or get a raise, it always ends the same – you become irritated with your job and have an overwhelmingly strong desire to leave.

This feeling that you feel, regardless of the job, is the feeling of being trapped by someone else. Unlike the 9 to 5er, you need freedom from organizational work entirely. You need to be your own boss. No job, no matter how great the company culture might be or how impressive the salary is, will ever be as fulfilling and enjoyable as working for yourself. Let this moment be the sign you have been waiting for to start your own business, podcast, brand, or blog. Life is too short to waste working for a company that will, in the end, negatively impact your life, your family's life, and your community. Take the leap and become your own boss.

The Road to Entrepreneurship

In 2015, a friend of mine graduated from university with a degree in graphic design and a certificate in advertising. As the hard worker she is, she was able to land a graphic design job immediately after college. After years of working for this multi-million-dollar company, she was unexpectedly laid off. Thankfully, she was able to continue developing and refining her design skills through freelancing and personal projects. Months later, and equipped with a refreshed portfolio, she was able to land her next job at a footwear company. Unfortunately, life happened, and she was sadly let go from said company. Desperate to pay the bills, she leaned heavily into freelancing projects until a new opportunity came along. And a new opportunity did! With the exciting news of motherhood presented to her, her eyes were finally opened to the fact that she needed to be a graphic design entrepreneur. With her sweet baby on the way, she couldn't continue to rely on mega-corporations to provide her with consistent income and flexibility. She found great success in freelancing on the side and in between periods of employment uncertainty, but now, after years of ups and downs, income disparity, and job ambiguity, she finally decided to leap into full-time freelance designing and has been flourishing ever since.

What about you? Is there something you have been doing on the side or even at your current place of work that you love doing that could transition into your own business? Utilizing the space below, write down a few things you enjoy doing that could be a great business opportunity.

_____

_____

_____

_____

_____

_____

_____

Leaving the 9 to 5

After some much-needed soul-searching, Jennifer realized that the problem wasn't her furry clients or the pet store itself that was causing her frustration; it was the concept of working for someone else. With this new understanding, Jennifer gave her two weeks' notice, said goodbye to her furry clients, packed her grooming tools, and set out to start her own pet grooming company.

In Chapter 7, we will discuss how to start your own business utilizing the tools from this Chapter and Chapter 2, but for now, I want you to begin to lay the foundations for your departure. Do you need to try to find someone to replace you in your current role so your current company can have a smooth transition, upon your departure? Do you need to start condensing and reorganizing your files to prepare them for whoever takes over your position? Maybe you don't need

"Life is too short to waste working for a company that will, in the end, negatively impact your life."

to do anything for your company but rather for yourself to feel secure enough to make the switch. Perhaps you need to utilize these next few paychecks to pay off debts so that you are financially okay until your business takes off, or you need to build up your savings to live off of while you build your brand. Whatever you need to do to make leaving your 9 to 5 a seamless transition, write it down.

_____

_____

_____

_____

_____

_____

_____

_____

_____

_____

_____

_____

_____

_____

_____

As you finish writing down your transitional list of tasks, let's discuss our final group, the non-traditional worker.

CHAPTER 5
The Non-Traditional Worker

It is said that being a parent or spouse is one of the most rewarding things a person can be. While society seems to be actively fighting against stay-at-home parents/spouses, you feel a strong calling to be at home and take care of your family and household. You are a non-traditional worker, and it's about time someone acknowledges that what you desire to do is just as important as the other two worker types.

Johnathan has worked in corporate America since the age of 18. He was taught that the ideal role for a man is to marry a beautiful woman, have some kids, and work a well-paying 9 to 5 job. Rather than wasting time in university, Johnathan decided to get a certificate in civil engineering and start his career early. By the age of 25, Johnathan had worked his way up the corporate ladder and was making six figures. He met the love of his life, Amy, married her, and together they had a beautiful daughter, Susana. Johnathan was a great dad. Every day, his little girl would cry as he left for work and would be overjoyed when he came home. Rather than spending the weekends with friends or nights with coworkers, Johnathan used every single bit of extra time he had to spend with Amy and their daughter. By the time Susana was three years old, Amy had given birth to a baby boy, Dylan. At the birth of Dylan, something clicked within Johnathan; he HATED working outside of the home. Sure, he was providing for his family, but deep down, Johnathan wanted to be a stay-at-home dad.

How Do You Know You Are Meant to Be a Non-Traditional Worker?

Like the other worker types, it all comes down to your personality. There are those whose personality types make them the perfect candidate for traditional employment, be it as a 9 to 5er or an entrepreneur, and then there are those whose personality is just right for being a non-traditional worker. Often, in society, these ideal personality traits are misunderstood to hint at a specific 9 to 5 job, such as teaching or nursing, but sometimes, these traits reveal a career field that many overlook: the career of being a stay-at-home parent/spouse.

Refer back to the personality assessment you took in Chapter 2. Did you notice that most of your natural traits are those of a caregiver? Have you ever thought, "Maybe I should be a teacher; I love kids," or "Nursing might be the best career for me; I love taking care of others?" When you go to work in the morning, do you wish you could stay home and make lunch for your kids or plan exciting weekend activities for your family? These dreams are those of a non-traditional worker. You have the personality to thrive in this worker type and desire to be the best at it, so why not take the leap and express your desires to your spouse? Who knows, they might surprise you and be on board with the idea.

Ready to have this difficult conversation with his wife, Johnathan sat down with Amy and expressed his interest in being a stay-at-home dad. Shocked by the nature of this conversation, Amy asked, "But why? We both have amazing jobs. Susana and Dylan are fine, and you love what you do. So why the sudden interest in being at home?"

Why Do You Want to Be a Non-Traditional Worker?

In addition to having a personality type centered around giving and caretaking, what you enjoy doing and how it will positively impact your family should also reflect your desire to be at home. Those who love cooking, cleaning, organizing, and planning activities will thrive as non-traditional workers. When asked why she wanted to be a stay-at-home mom, a friend of mine stated that choosing the family meals, picking out the ingredients, and cooking the food was one thing she really enjoyed. It perfectly combined her caregiver personality with her love for organic and healthy food and her interest in cooking while simultaneously promoting healthy habits for her husband and daughter.

With a look of concern and confusion on her face, Amy awaited her husband's answer. After taking a deep breath, Johnathan replied, "Well, I have three reasons for doing this, and they all will benefit our family in the long run: Reason #1, our children. Children need consistency at home to feel safe to go out and explore. Every time we drop them off at daycare or school, we are causing emotional whiplash that is only going to develop negative habits as they get older. Children need to grow up in a stable and dependable environment; they need to know that it is okay to go out and explore because one of us will always be there as a lifeline should they need it. Right now, we are already seeing the negative effects of not being consistently there with Susana. Whenever we pick her up from school, she doesn't leave our side until we force her back to school the next day. She spends 8 hours away from us, being thrown from classroom to classroom, teacher to teacher. Sure, she is on a schedule, but she isn't confident in trying new things or meeting new people when we're around because she's scared we'll leave her, just like we do every day – Monday through Friday. We have failed her in these first five years of her life. I don't want to keep failing her, nor do I want to start the same cycle with Dylan."

One of the major reasons why many feel a calling to be a non-traditional worker is their children. Studies have shown that children raised by stay-at-home parents are more likely to excel in school, succeed in life, and thrive in their careers. They are more confident and courageous. They aren't afraid to stand up for what is good and are most willing to fight for what's right. Because of the stay-at-home parent commitment, their children will know their self-worth and are far less likely to be involved in destructive relationships, work for horrible bosses, or seek affirmation from non-reliable sources.

Surprised by the passionate tone in her husband's voice, Amy replied, "You're right. I have noticed that as well. Okay, you said you have three reasons; what's the second?" Encouraged by his wife's openness, Johnathan continued with his second reason. "Reason #2: I'd like to be the leader of the home, in the home. Planning family bonding activities, creating schedules, organizing the home, and establishing a healthy home life will give you and the children a safe place to excel. I've been reading a lot about how different home layouts can affect the success of those who live there. Rather than utilizing my expertise in engineering for some company that doesn't value me, I'd rather use it to create an environment that will help our children grow and help you succeed in your career.

It's no surprise that what you enjoy doing could easily pivot from a 9 to 5 or entrepreneur worker type to a non-traditional worker type. Regardless of which category you fall into, when you do what you enjoy, you will naturally thrive, be excited, and be motivated to do it well. As a non-traditional worker, it's essential to think about what you like to do and present it as a benefit to your partner as a justifiable reason to become a non-traditional worker. In Johnathan's case, he loves civil engineering. He has a proven track record of excelling in his career. As an engineer, he has noticed various things in his home that need to be updated. The structure and layout of his home are not conducive to a creative and inspiring environment. If he were to be a non-traditional worker, he could make the necessary updates to the home that would allow his family to flourish in their various activities without breaking the bank. This is an excellent benefit for Amy, as she is a lawyer, and having a home that is favorable to the type of work she does would greatly benefit her.

With a nod of agreement, Amy looked at her husband and said, "You know, having you use your engineering skills to enhance our home would be amazing. Honestly, it would be great for the kids to learn valuable life skills from you rather than in public school. But before we make any final decisions, what was your third reason?" With a deep breath, Johnathan took his wife's hand and said,

"When you do what you enjoy, you will naturally thrive, be excited, and be motivated to do well."

"The final reason is you." "I know how much it bothers you that neither of us can be with our kids all day. I see the frustration of balancing your career and raising our kids. I know that you are meant to be a 9 to 5er. You light up every time you talk about a new case or a new piece of evidence that you've uncovered. Let me take over the responsibilities of our home so that you can focus on being the best lawyer this city has ever seen."

Being able to speak to how operating as a non-traditional worker will positively impact the traditional worker will significantly increase your chances of them being on board with this idea. Think about the areas in your partner's life that would benefit the most from you taking on the non-traditional worker role and present that to them during the conversation.

With a sparkle in her eyes, Amy replied, "Okay, let's try it. Let me know how I can help you transition from your job to being a stay-at-home dad."

CHAPTER 6

Setting the Foundation
(The 9 to 5er)

With a completed personality assessment, an understanding of the type of work environment in which he thrives, and an excitement for what he enjoys doing, Jeremy is ready to start his new and fulfilling 9-to-5 career.

One of the best places to start when thinking about your next 9-to-5 opportunity is with what you enjoy doing. In Jeremy's case, he enjoys sports, specifically football. Here, Jeremy will begin his research by looking at various job opportunities that will allow him to work with or in sports, ideally in football.

Similar to Jeremy, a friend of mine had gotten her law degree, thinking that law was the path to success for her. While completing her degree, her love of writing blossomed into something that could no longer take a backseat in her life. Fulfilling her obligation to her family, she completed her pre-law degree. Still, her heart longed to be a writer, so she took a chance and started looking for writing opportunities to build her portfolio.

Like Jeremy and my friend, there is something that you genuinely enjoy doing, something that makes your day better when given the time and space to do it. In Chapter

3, you wrote down a few things that bring you joy. Take that list and begin considering what job opportunities will allow you to do what you love. Maybe you are a foodie and long for a career centered around food. A few job options for you could be a chef, a food blogger for a well-known cooking magazine/blog, a professional food critic, or a caterer. Whatever activities you wrote down in Chapter 3, write down a few related jobs that will pay you to do what enjoy.

The Right Job for Your Personality Type

In Chapter 2, we introduced the concept of finding a job that aligns with your personality type. Although it is important to have a job that incorporates things you enjoy, it could all be for nothing if you're outside of your personality type. Take my former co-worker, for example. She loves fashion, style, and, most of all, shopping. Starting as a business manager, she quickly moved into the visual manager role at a department store. Although she was doing what she enjoyed, fashion, she was miserable. The visual manager role at the department store was more of a hands-off approach with customers. The job was to make the store visually appealing and coach the team to the standards of the corporate office.

Even though she excelled at her job, my former co-worker was outside of her personality type. Have you guessed what her personality type is yet? She's an extrovert. She loves interacting with people, styling clients, and sharing her fashion sense with anyone who would listen. As the visual manager, creating a personal connection with shoppers was something that she could not do. Finally fed up with her job, she gave her notice, packed her things, and moved to a new city. There, she found the perfect job at a small boutique. In her new role, she was given the opportunity to work as a buyer for the boutique (utilizing her love of shopping), remerchandise the store and style mannequins (utilizing her love of fashion and style), and interact with clientele daily (utilizing her extroverted personality). Although it took a little bit of hard work and determination to get there, she was finally doing a job that aligned with her personality type and what she enjoyed.

Reflect on the results of your personality assessment. What are the key traits you discovered about yourself that align with the potential jobs list from earlier? Perhaps you're an introvert with a passion for fashion or an extrovert who enjoys video games. Whatever your interests are, compare them against the jobs that align with your personality type.

The Ultimate Workplace Environment

We understand that our mental and physical health should never be compromised for a job, career, or paycheck. Chapter 3 emphasized the importance of finding a workplace environment that aligns with your values, treats you with dignity, and doesn't inflict harm upon you. Alongside these fundamental aspects, there are specific elements that you personally look for in your ideal work environment.

Based on the activities completed in this book, Jeremy knows he is looking for a sports-related job, ideally in football, that will allow him to be detail-oriented, interact with people, and be creative. He has determined that working for a sports marketing firm is most likely the best job for him, as it combines his love of sports with his personality type. Now, a huge question is raised: which marketing firm should he pursue? This is where knowing the workplace environment comes into effect.

In Chapter 3, you wrote down a list of workplace attributes you want in your next 9 to 5, as well as some attributes you wish to avoid. Utilizing your list of dos and don'ts, cross-reference them with the list of companies you made in the last section. Websites like Glassdoor and Google Reviews are great resources for seeing what current and former employees say about the company(s) you are considering. LinkedIn is another great resource, as you can connect with former and current employees and ask them directly about their experience with XYZ company. A word of caution: some former employees may have animosity toward the business, so cross-reference reviews and testimonials with various sources to get the most accurate information.

After much research, Jeremy finally completed his list of the top 10 most ideal companies to work for and was ready to move forward and start applying.

CHAPTER 7

Landing the Job & Thriving

I'm sure by now you are ready to turn in your keys and start your new career as a free 9 to 5er. You've taken the necessary steps, and you have your list of ideal companies ready to go. All that's left is to apply.

Applying for a job that you desperately want is challenging in itself. Add in a change of career, and things really start to look scary. But fret not; the hard part is over. You know exactly where you want to work. You have the experience from previous employers to show your qualifications, a passion for the area you find enjoyable, and the determination to work hard in this new role, as proven by the completed activities in this book. The first step in applying for your ideal career is creating the perfect resume for that company. Notice that I said for that company, not for that industry. To truly stand out, your resume should speak to the company you are applying for. There are many HR representatives, resume builders, and hiring managers who constantly reiterate this sentiment, "if you want your resume to stand out, it needs to align with the attributes the company is looking for, not just what the general industry requires.

A great way to start building your resume is through the job itself. In Jeremy's case, he needs to build a resume that will be appealing to a recruiter at the sports marketing company he is interested in. His resume should include key actions such as successful projects he has worked on in the past, how detail-oriented he is, and times he has done something with sports. After the foundation is laid, Jeremy needs to modify his resume based on the needs of the specific company he is applying to. One company might need to see more numerical results, so Jeremy will highlight how his actions in previous roles positively impacted the numbers at his former employer. Another company may need more of a creative person to join their sports marketing team; in this case, Jeremy will want to hone in on his more creative projects and the positive impact they had on the company's goals. Regardless of the job, it's imperative that your resume aligns with the needs of the business.

Start Applying

Having the perfect resume means nothing if you don't actually apply for the job(s) you've worked so hard in researching and prepping for. Keep in mind, the goal is freedom in the 9 to 5, not to be trapped until the other 9 to 5 decides to release you; case and point, a friend and former coworker of mine.

My friend and former coworker has a personality type that is perfect for customer service. In fact, she has said on numerous occasions that she loves taking care of customers, just not at the place she is currently working. Her dream is to be a nail tech. Not only does she have the skills to do so, but many of the customers she has interacted with at her current job have asked if she was able to take them as clients.

After several conversations with her about how much she would like to leave her employer and pursue a career as a nail tech, I decided to do some research to help her get started. Upon gaining insight and clarity from my personal nail tech, I shared clear step-by-step instructions with her on how to start doing nails professionally and leave her current place of work. I was able to set up an arrangement with the salon that would have allowed her to work and learn firsthand while studying to get her cosmetology license, with a guaranteed job as a nail tech upon graduation.

"The goal is freedom in the 9 to 5, not to be trapped until the other 9 to 5 decides to release you."

The plan seemed to be simple, easy, and perfect for her; but like many others, the unknown world of changing jobs and doing something you love is scary. Unfortunately, despite my best efforts, she is still working at the company she longed to depart from to this day. And what's even worse, not only did they not recognize her for her talent, hard work, and dedication to customer service, but they gave her a massive pay cut, increased responsibility, and a work environment that can only be described as volatile and unpredictable.

Don't be like my friend. Take the necessary steps to change to a different 9 to 5; one that aligns with the benefits you look for in a company, values and respects you, and will reward you for the effort you put into your job.

The Interview

Congratulations! Your resume was accepted, and now it's time for your interview. What an exciting moment! You are one step closer to experiencing workplace freedom.

Sitting down in an interview can be nerve-racking for some, especially for a job you want. One technique to overcome interviewing fears is preparing examples that show a positive correlation between the job and your skill set. Take a look at Jeremy, he has done his research on the company, the job, and the recruiter. With his new information, he can cross-reference against his skills, expertise, and experience. After reaching out to current and past employees, he has a better understanding of the work culture and environment and will be able to refer back to previous jobs with a similar culture.

Knowing the intricate details of the job, the company, and the overall industry will give you the confidence to answer nearly any question the interviewer may have. I will, however, advise against practicing interview questions beforehand, as this could lead to rigid answers and stiffened body language. Instead, you want to be bold and confident in your answers. Let your personality be the connection between you and the interviewer, your experience be the connection between you and the job, and your expertise be the connection between you and the company.

Establishing Healthy Boundaries

Although it's important to be 100% dedicated to the craft and work diligently towards excellence within your role, providing your undying loyalty to one company is utterly insane. The sad reality is that even the best companies have the capability of terminating their best employees to save a few bucks. Therefore, rule #1 is not to commit 1000% of yourself to a company that is only willing to commit 1% to you.

You are an asset to the team and to the company. Being committed to your expertise and refining your skills is what makes you valuable in this role, not your complete surrender and dedication to the company. Establishing a healthy boundary between committing to the job and committing to the company is one of the most important things you can do when you first start a new job.

"Rule #1: Do not commit 1000% of yourself to a company that is only willing to commit 1% to you."

A common theme amongst 9 to 5ers is the need to BECOME their job. They confuse the tasks of their job with who they are as a person, often believing that without this specific job, they are nothing. Of course, this couldn't be further from the truth. You are not your job; you are a lawyer, a chef, a designer, a computer genius, or an influencer. Your skills and attributes do not confine you to your current employer; you are free to take who you are and your skills and use them in whatever worker type you want. Rule #2: always remember that a job is a job and not who you are.

Do you remember my graphic design friend? She understood this concept. Not only had she been designing since she was a child, but she also obtained a degree in graphic design. Despite losing her first out-of-college job and being let go from her next corporate gig, she continued to pursue graphic design until she became a full-time freelancer. In her case, a job was simply just a job, but being a graphic designer, that's who she is. Whether working for a corporation or working for herself, you will always find her doing some kind of graphic design work.

"Rule #2: Always remember that a job is a job and not who you are"

Know Your Worth & Never Be Afraid to Leave

Rule #3, a rule that many 9 to 5ers struggle with, is the idea that you can't leave your job too soon. The argument is always the same: "You can't leave yet. You've only been here for less than a year! It looks really bad on your resume. Just stick it out a little longer so that your resume doesn't show your lack of commitment." Let me tell you, that's complete nonsense. I've known many people, including myself, who left their jobs after less than 6 months for various reasons. Don't subject yourself to unnecessary torture for the sake of your resume.

You deserve to be treated with respect and dignity. You don't deserve to work for a place that is dishonest and baited you into the role. You are a hard worker and should work for a company that not only recognizes this but honors it.

"Rule #3: If a company is harming you, no matter how short of a time you may have been employed, leave."

Don't be afraid to put your well-being above the well-being of someone else's business. As I used to tell my former manager, "Take care of yourself. What good are you to your loved ones and even this company if you're not well?" The same is true for you. Take care of yourself, and if a company is harming you, no matter how short of a time you may have been employed, leave – leave and never look back.

CHAPTER 8
Setting the Foundation
(The Entrepreneur)

Freedom as an entrepreneur is somewhat similar to freedom as a 9 to 5er but with one major difference: here, you are your own boss. You've considered the pros and cons of working for someone else and have decided it's better to invest in your business than in someone else's. After completing the personality assessment in Chapter 2 and rediscovering what you enjoy doing in Chapter 4, we are ready to begin building our ideal business.

What's Missing in Our World?

Do you know what makes an entrepreneur? It's the ability to see a problem in society and come up with a solution to fix it. Some of the best entrepreneurs in the world can rectify a problem in society and boost the economy. When you look at society, your neighborhood, or your community as a whole, where do you see a lack? Is there an area that makes you say, "Ugh! This is terrible! I wish I could do something to fix it!" Let's take a moment and go back to my graphic designer friend.

As you may recall, after many crazy life events, she finally decided to pursue freelance graphic designing as a full-time career, gaining clients and supporting her family. But what void or problem is she fixing as a freelance graphic designer? Surely, there are existing design agencies that can meet the needs of the market, so what makes her business so special? That's it! The fact that she isn't a design or marketing agency is what makes her business special. Have you ever taken the time to research how much hiring a design agency costs? It could cost an individual or business thousands of dollars for just one logo design. If you're a small business or entrepreneur, you may not have the kind of capital needed to invest in a Fortune 500 design agency yet; however, you still might want a professional to handle some or all of the graphic design aspects of your company. This is the void that my friends' business is filling. As a graphic design entrepreneur, she can tailor her pricing on a client-by-client basis rather than on a package-by-package basis, like most design companies. She can set her own schedule and take on as many or as few clients as she desires, which in turn will allow her the flexibility to bring in income and be a stay-at-home mom.

Now, it's your turn! Have you thought about the needs of society and where you feel the most drawn? Is there something that you have been doing all along that just now clicked that maybe this thing should be your business? Whatever it is, write it down!

Developing YOUR Business Concept

While important, understanding the community's needs is only the first step in developing your business. The next step is to cross-reference those needs with what you are good at. For example, let's say that you see a need to help homeless animals, but you don't like animals. It would not be wise to open an animal shelter, knowing that you and the animals don't get along. Instead, it would be better to donate to an existing shelter that is already helping the homeless animals and let them know whenever you see one when you're out and about.

If your business is going to thrive whilst fulfilling a need in society, it needs to be a business that you will enjoy having. Having a passion for cooking is not going to help a business that's all about cleaning. In Chapter 4, we talked about looking at things that we enjoy doing that COULD turn into a lucrative business. Utilizing that list, think about which areas from the "lacks" list could be positively impacted if your passions were turned into a business. Maybe you love sports and see that children in your community don't have anything to do after school or during the summer. Maybe you love to cook and notice there are a lot of small businesses in your area that are spending WAY too much money on big corporate caterers. Or maybe you love fashion and have noticed there aren't that many modest clothing brands out there. Whatever your interests are, cross-reference them with the needs of the community to see which of your passions could turn into a viable business.

It's YOU That Makes the Business

With the core foundation laid and an understanding of which needs in the market can be fulfilled through utilizing our passions, the final step in creating our business is incorporating who we are. In Chapter 2, you took a personality assessment that showed you a more in-depth look at yourself. Knowing your personality type will help to ensure that you are doing what you love and helping the community without burnout and indirect self-harm.

After completing the actions in this chapter, Jennifer discovered that there is a need for a traveling pet groomer in her community. She already loved animals and knew the proper techniques for a quality grooming service. She had taken the personality assessment years ago and knew that she was very introverted. Therefore, running a business that allows her the freedom and flexibility to set her own schedule, pick up and drop off her furry clients with minimal yet personal interaction with the owners, and groom and care for the clients her way, is ideal business.

I hope at this point in the book you are more like Jennifer. You know what you enjoy doing, have a deeper understanding of yourself, and have discovered a need in the market, society, or your community that you are capable of fulfilling through entrepreneurship. Maybe you love being in a quiet place alone with a good book and tea, but you also have the personality type to serve; opening a tranquil coffee and tea shop with vintage books for rent might be the perfect business for you. Maybe you love to play video games and cook, and your personality is one of planning and hosting; operating a business where fellow gamers can come together, play, and socialize over a delicious meal might be right up your alley. Take what you have learned about yourself, what you enjoy, and the needs of the market, and start to think about some business ideas you can flush out to make your dreams a reality.

CHAPTER 9

In Order to Succeed, You MUST Overcome

Seeing how vast the sea of competition is can be very discouraging and disheartening for an entrepreneur. You might think to yourself, "I've taken the steps in this book. I've taken online courses, and I've followed the advice of those before me, but there seem to be so many people in my market that I just don't think I am good enough. Maybe I should give up and stay at my current job; at least that's stable." First of all, if this is how you rationalize staying with your current employer, let this be the sign that you are being held captive and need to be set free from that place.

Secondly, there is no such thing as "too much competition." Business competition is great! It shows that there is a need in the market for this or that. It shows that there is a customer or audience that is willing and able to buy your product or service. All you have to do is find what makes you different from everyone else. Why should the consumer shop your brand, watch your YouTube videos, or subscribe to your service? The answer? Because you have created a business based on the needs of the market, you looked at the beauty industry and saw that there is a problem that no one else has solved yet. You've taken your passion for storytelling and created a business that invites others to express themselves through the art of writing. You've honed in on your personality type and started a business that takes advantage of who you are and helps others become the best versions of themselves. Competition isn't bad. It's not something to shy away from. All it does is reinforce the truth that there are customers out there willing to buy your service or product; you just need to apply what you have learned thus far to an area within the market that is lacking.

Although concurring the fear of competition can be difficult, there is no obstacle more difficult to overcome than overcoming yourself. Self-doubt is the death of every entrepreneurial idea and business concept. If you don't believe in yourself, your product, or your service, no one will. I know, more than anyone, how hard it is to believe in yourself and your business. I have always had a heart for business and helping people. I am also very creative, and I love fashion. When I was younger, I thought the fashion industry was where I was destined to be. From the wild designs of Project Runway to the glitz and glam of America's Next Top Model to the client transformations of What Not to Wear, I wanted all of it, and gosh darn it, I was going to have it! At a young age, I tried my hand at entrepreneurship. Designing and making blankets for people and learning how to design clothes, hoping to open a boutique one day. With the support of my parents, I continued my path into entrepreneurship by completing my certificates in apparel design and business by the age of 17 and graduating from university with a degree in business management & entrepreneurship. With two great internships under my belt and a college degree in hand, I was headed out into the world, ready to embark on a journey that would allow me to combine my love of fashion, my love of business, and my heart to help others.

Self-doubt immediately hit me the moment I graduated. Rather than utilizing the degree I worked so hard for to open my own business, I decided to work for a clothing company as a manager in training, thinking that maybe this is a better career path than starting my own company. A year into that career path, things took a dramatic turn, and I knew I needed to leave that place of work. Although my managers were great, and I was making great connections

"Self-doubt is the death of every entrepreneurial idea and business."

with shoppers, I knew there was something more than this. Something didn't feel right about this career path. So, I packed my bags, moved to Spain, and became an English Teacher. "Um! Excuse me?!?!?" I hear you saying. "What do you mean English Teacher? That has nothing to do with what you were doing, nor with what you wanted to do, or even what you are doing now!" Right, right. I know it sounds crazy. And you're right, teaching has nothing to do with my degree, what I wanted to do, or even what I am doing now. But in that season of my life, I needed a hard reset, and let me tell you I got it!

While living in Spain, in between teaching and tutoring, I was given the opportunity to work as a virtual stylist for a start-up project. It was so much fun! Never in my career had I ever had a job that let me live abroad, work remotely, choose my schedule, and style people. It was almost the perfect job. I loved that job so much that I quit teaching intending to work full-time as a virtual stylist. Isn't it funny how, just when you think you have it all figured out, the Lord allows a little annoyance to throw off your plans? Remember, my heart is that of an entrepreneur, not one of a 9 to 5er. Even though I was gung-ho about working for this company and living forever in Spain as a virtual stylist, the Lord sent a little nudge to push me to the path I was supposed to be on. What was that nudge, you may be asking? Oh, it was the project shutting down, leading to the firing of every single virtual stylist who worked there, including myself.

Even though my virtual stylist career with this particular company had come to an end, I was still determined to do something similar. I had tasted what freedom in the workplace was like, and I wanted nothing more than to have it again. After two years of living my best life in Spain, I came back to the US with a single plan in mind: start my own styling company and move back to Spain ASAP. Well, dear reader, that plan did not happen. Within a year of being back in the US, I, along with the rest of the world, was slapped in the face by the pandemic! Yikes… talk about "freedom". Imagine going from living in a country all by yourself with plans of working an amazing job to having no job and living with your parents, siblings, pets, and a baby in less than three years. Quite jarring if I do say so myself. Even though the situation was less than ideal, I was finally pushed back to the path I had strayed from all of those years ago. Rather than being miserable and annoyed by the pandemic, I decided to take all of that energy and start my own styling company.

Self-doubt can truly delay a good thing. Had I stayed the course and not allowed the influence of those around me in college to cloud my mind, I could have started my business earlier than I did. But I allowed myself to make excuses and create reasons as to why I needed to wait to start, why I needed more information or more resources. I used those years after college to delay my calling and my purpose instead of using that time to get a jump start on fulfilling my destiny. As much as I would love to sit here and tell you that I learned my lesson, and once I started my styling business, it was all uphill from there, I simply cannot, as that would not be entirely true. Unfortunately, the self-doubt came back around year three of my business.

It's Going to Be Hard, Don't Give Up!

The fear of not succeeding and self-doubt will always try to rear its ugly head whenever you are taking a chance on yourself. What's important, in that moment, is to not let it win. Remember, you're an entrepreneur! You've found a need in the market that you're passionate about fixing. You've done the research and figured out how to combine your passions with fixing a problem and are steadfast in making a new and better life for yourself and your community. Fear and doubt will always try to derail you, especially when things are starting to look up. How do I know? Oh, because that is exactly what happened to me. I allowed fear and doubt to enter my mind and derail my plans, just when my business was finally taking off.

Around year three of running my styling company, things started to gain momentum. I was getting new clients, posting more frequently on social media, and even started a YouTube channel. At last, I was combining my love of fashion and business, and I was on my way to experiencing that freedom in the workplace I so desperately desired.

Despite knowing that entrepreneurship was the best path for me, I decided to pause my business and focus my efforts on making as much money as possible as quickly as possible. Rather than being committed to my purpose, I chose to work for several different companies in a very short time frame.

Like many entrepreneurs trying to find their way, maybe you've decided that it's better to just stay at your current job instead of pursuing your dreams. Maybe you feel that it's easier to just work a 9 to 5 and hope that things will get better. Let me tell you firsthand that going that route is not only a waste of time, but it will make you absolutely miserable in the end. My hope is that this book will encourage you to not make the same mistake that I did – wasting so much precious time working for companies that don't value you, don't fulfill you, and don't bring you joy. Learn from my mistakes. It's never too late to make a hard stop and

"The fear of not succeeding and self-doubt will always try to rear its ugly head whenever you are taking a chance on yourself."

pivot away from the madness of the toxic 9 to 5 and towards the free life of an entrepreneur that you've always wanted.

If You Fail, Get Back Up and Try Again

Like you, being a business owner/entrepreneur is something that I was destined to be, and helping people has always been at the core of my purpose. Looking over the course of my life, one thing has always been consistent. No matter if it's school, work, or random conversations in a coffee shop, I constantly find ways to dig into a person's life, discover that they are unhappy with where they are, and provide them with encouragement and resources to free them from whatever was keeping them from their destiny. Whether it was helping women display their inner beauty of the outside through my styling company, or helping all worker types experience a new kind of workplace freedom, my calling in life is to help those who feel captive, be it by society, work, or some other third thing, experience a freedom they thought was only a dream. I may have failed, stumbled, and at times given up, but by the grace of God, the help of my family, and the support of my friends I was able to get back up and try again. Allow me to encourage you as well.

Maybe you've failed at your business, maybe you gave up, or maybe you never even tried; let this moment be the encouragement that you need to get up and start again. The only guaranteed way to not succeed in the life of entrepreneurship is to give up and never try again. Don't be that person. You can do it! Start from scratch if you need to. I believe in you, I'm praying for you, and I'm rooting for you! You've got this. Your business will be a success. And you WILL experience a new freedom in life through entrepreneurship. Now go out there and be great!

CHAPTER 10

Setting the Foundation
(The Non-Traditional Worker)

In Chapter 5, you learned about yourself, through the personality assessment, and wrote down a list of reasons why you want to be a non-traditional worker. To excel in this role, you must combine the information from Chapter 5 with your list of things that you enjoy doing. Maybe you discovered that you have the personality type to grow, nurture, and cultivate things; but also have an interest in healthy eating and habits. In this case, maybe starting a garden of fresh fruits and vegetables is the perfect way to feed your family, contribute to the household, and do something that you enjoy. Take a moment and think about how you can combine your personality type with what you like to do and how that combination will be of benefit to your family and home.

Personality Type	+ Enjoyment	= Family Benefit
Detailed-Oriented	*Planning Events*	*Hosting the best celebrations for the family*

Being the Best Non-Traditional Worker You Can Be

Let's go back to Johnathan and his family, for a moment. The core foundation for why Johnathan wanted to be a stay-at-home dad was his children. He wanted to directly impact the lives of his children through raising them firsthand. Granted, being a stay-at-home dad wasn't in his original life plan, but nevertheless, he was determined to be the best stay-at-home dad he could be.

Whether it's raising children or being a homemaker, it's important to obtain as much information as possible in order to excel as a non-traditional worker. Combining your personality type with what you enjoy doing, plus focusing on the benefits for your family, is only the beginning step to succeeding as a non-traditional worker. The next step is to obtain as much information as possible regarding your goals as a stay-at-home spouse/parent. In Johnathan's case, his goal was to raise children that are hard-working, passionate, and positive contributors to society. He hopes to utilize his skills and experience in civil engineering to teach his children useful life lessons.

As a man, he hopes to show his son how a man ought to carry himself within society and show his daughter how she should be treated by her future husband. Although his motives are pure and his goals are clear, he lacks some key information on how to accomplish his objectives.

Books and online resources are a great starting place when it comes to obtaining information. Be it parenting, relationships, cooking, or cleaning; there is a book out there that will guide you towards success as a non-traditional worker. Take a moment to write down a few goals you want to meet as a non-traditional worker. Maybe you want to be the best stay-at-home parent, like Johnathan, or maybe you want to promote a healthy lifestyle like my friend; whatever your goals are, write them down and see if there is any overlap between your goals and how the family will benefit from you staying at home.

_____

_____

_____

Looking at the lists, are there any areas in which you lack knowledge? Maybe you decided that as a stay-at-home spouse, your goal is to create a home environment that will aid in the success of your traditional working spouse. Although you are good at designing and have a detail-oriented personality, you lack the fundamental skills to execute your goal. Additional resources are key to the success of being a non-traditional worker. Take some time and research materials that will aid you in the areas you are lacking.

For our stay-at-home spouses, being child-free definitely has its perks; one of which is being able to focus 100% on enhancing the household. Maybe you have a passion for building and creating, but rather than being your own boss or working for a company, you'd rather utilize your skills at home. Does the entrepreneur need a new office space to work in? Great! You are free to remodel a room into the perfect office. Does your 9 to 5er need a quiet place to rest after a long day? Wonderful! As a stay-at-home spouse, you are free to utilize your skills of building and love of creativity to cultivate the perfect relaxation room within your home. Take a moment to think about how you can utilize what you love to do to bring value into your home.

Supporting the Traditional Worker

All of the books, courses, and information will be utterly useless if the traditional worker is unable to successfully provide sufficient income. Being the sole financial provider for the household can be quite burdensome for the traditional worker. Don't get me wrong, this is what they are meant to do. As a 9 to 5er or entrepreneur, it brings them great joy to be able to provide income for the family. Even though they are delighted to do it, it doesn't mean it's easy. Part of being a non-traditional worker is the ability to aid in the success of the traditional worker. It means being there for them when they need it. It means providing emotional, spiritual, mental, and sometimes, physical support. It means maintaining the home so that the traditional worker can focus on providing financial aid to you and your family. You are the foundation for the traditional worker, and your support are the building blocks to a successful partnership.

I had the pleasure of interviewing my friend's husband for this book. Like many husbands, he has taken on the role of traditional worker, specifically a 9 to 5er. Of course, being a traditional worker is tough, so with a beautiful daughter and a loving wife at home, I wanted to know how his wife supports him as he provides monetarily for his family.

1) Raising Their Daughter: One of the major contributions from his wife is staying home to raise their daughter full-time. Although she has a degree in architecture and a master's in teaching, she decided to step away from traditional work and dedicate her life to working for her family, as both a stay-at-home mom and wife. In doing this, he can focus on doing his very best at work without fear or concern for his daughter's safety with an unknown third party.

2) Creating & Establishing Healthy Habits: His wife has a passion for a healthy lifestyle. Be it eating organic foods, meditating, or getting fresh air; she is always looking for new ways to promote a natural way of life. This is another benefit for him. Because she works diligently to provide healthy foods, a safe space to unwind and relax, and an excitement for nature, he can decompress after a hard day of work without needing a harmful vise.

3) Being a Positive Foundation: Lastly, she has become a positive foundation in his life. She diligently reminds him to maintain his morning routines, as they have positively impacted his mental and physical health. She shares encouraging ideas and concepts to help him fight against harmful thoughts and feelings. Most importantly, she reassures him of the benefits of his job. Whenever there is a bad day, annoying meeting, or frustrating task, she is there to remind him of all of the good that he does in his job and encourage him to keep going, despite the frustrations of the day.

As a non-traditional worker, what are some ways you can support and encourage your traditionally working spouse? Take a moment and sit down with your partner and ask them how you can support them as they pursue their 9 to 5 job or business. You are the key to their success. If they are successful, you are successful. It's a team effort!

CHAPTER 11
Finally Free

We've talked about how to know if you need to be free, what kind of worker you are, and how to get started in your ideal worker type, now it's time to talk about the part that we've all been waiting for… "When can I finally quit my job?"

Goodbye, Captivity…

With all of the prep from this book complete, it's time to quit your job the moment you find a new 9 to 5, the moment your business is making enough money to support you and itself, the moment your partner can comfortably support you and your family. The last thing we want is to jump from one stress to another. We're talking about freedom, not transferred captivity. Leaving your 9 to 5 without having a solid financial foundation to land on is only going to cause stress, frustrations, and financial ruin. I know every financial guru out there says to quit your job right now and start your business, and although I am no guru, I am telling you that is the absolute worst thing you could do for yourself, your business, and your family. Take it slow and responsibly; solidify your new job, and your business, or wait for your spouse to become financially stable, and then move away from your 9 to 5. This will ensure a smooth financial transition for you and eliminate any unnecessary hardship.

... Hello, Freedom

Whether you're a 9 to 5er looking for the perfect 9 to 5 job, an entrepreneur ready to start your own business, or a non-traditional worker eager to pour your skills into your home, I hope that the contents of this book inspired you to take the necessary steps into worker freedom. Life is too short to work in captivity! You deserve to do what you were created to do and live a fulfilling life.

Thank you again for taking the time to read this book. I truly hope that I was able to inspire, encourage, and excite you into transitioning from captivity into worker freedom. It breaks my heart to see so many people barely living life, enslaved to the dreadful 9 to 5, and neglecting their mental health. I hope that through this book people can experience a fulfilling life, where bills are paid, dreams come true, and families are happy. Thank you once more for your trust in me as you begin this new journey through life as a free worker.

ABOUT THE AUTHOR

Victoria Jarvis, author and podcaster, loves God, coffee, and helping people find enjoyment in their lives. After graduating with a degree in Business Management and Entrepreneurship, completing two fashion internships, and nearly a decade of working within the fashion retail space, Victoria began embarking on a new journey to help those held captive by their job find freedom in the workplace. Be it as the 9-to-5er, entrepreneur, or non-traditional worker, Victoria believes everyone can enjoy the benefits of working if given the right tools.

In addition to this book, you can learn more about how to experience freedom in the workplace on her podcast *Coffee with Torie* available on YouTube and other podcasting platforms.

ADDITIONAL PAGES

www.ingramcontent.com/pod-product-compliance
Lightning Source LLC
Chambersburg PA
CBHW071831210526
45479CB00001B/80